Joy of Every Longing Heart

*An Advent of
Expectation and Rejoicing
for Weary Hearts*

Casey Martin

In *Joy of Every Longing Heart*, the audience is drawn toward deep spiritual truth in a season with so much noise. It is a catalyst for purifying, comforting, and guarding the weary heart during such a tender time of year. Walking through Casey's advent in the context of community was a powerful experience and will be an ongoing tradition.

Brooke Talley
Founder of Songs in the Night

Joy of Every Longing Heart is a gift to the grieving during the Holiday Season! Christmas can be a very difficult time of year for the griever, and Casey reminds us that not only are we understood in the mixed emotions we feel, but that we are also not alone! I would encourage all who are grieving to allow this devotional to speak to their aching hearts as it encourages you each and every day to keep your eyes on the Ultimate Gift at Christmas, the Hope we have in Jesus!

Jeff and Mackenzie Rollins
Founders of Hope Family Care Ministries

The holidays have a way of magnifying pain for those who are weary. In *Joy of Every Longing Heart*, Casey shares her journey of suffering with a raw vulnerability that assures readers they are not alone. In each daily reading, Casey acknowledges that while pain is present, so too is Jesus; and thus, the unexpected possibility of joy. If you or someone you love is hurting this holiday season, this book is the perfect gift.

Kelli Wild, LCSW
Therapist and founder of Soul Care for Weary Parents

Contents

Introduction

It was Thanksgiving Day, and I was standing on the hard cold earth of my daughter's grave. An entire year had not yet passed since her unexpected death; we were entering our first Christmas season without her. I didn't feel very thankful, and I wasn't looking forward to returning home to set up festive decorations. Tears streamed down my face, and I repeated a now-familiar prayer, "Jesus, please be near."

Time marched on, and I found myself amid the typical hustle and bustle that the holiday season brings. The usual holiday cheer felt abrasive, and my longing for Jesus intensified. There is so much hope and joy to be celebrated in the Christmas story, but the typical fanfare seemed to mock my pain instead of usher me to the throne room of the King.

Psalm 56:8 says, "You yourself have recorded my wanderings. Put my tears in your bottle. Are they not in your book?" God knows our pain and the longing of our hearts. I long for Jesus amid the hurt of this world, and I long for the King who will come again, making all things new. Grief has not dulled the celebrations surrounding Christmas; it has illuminated the majesty of Jesus.

Dear friend, if I could sit and have coffee with you, these are the words I would share. Maybe you know the sting of death, face a poor health diagnosis, or feel abandoned. Perhaps loss is fresh, and grief is heavy. Possibly, you feel out of place in the world around you. Suffering can be lonely. While I can't know or understand the circumstances you wake to each morning, Jesus knows and understands.

Isaiah 53:3 tells us, "He was despised and rejected by men, a man of suffering who knew what sickness was. He was like someone people turned away from; he was despised, and we didn't value him."

This Christmas, I encourage you to set traditions aside if need be and enter humbly to sit at the feet of Jesus. Sit with gratitude for what Christ has done and wait with expectation for all he has yet to do. Each day of this Advent will provide a short devotion, questions to ponder, and Scripture to meditate on more fully. Let these exercises in expectation spur you to plunge even deeper into the fullness of God's Word. There is joy to be found amid longing, and you will find it with Jesus.

Come, Thou Long Expected Jesus

December 1

"Look on the bright side" might be one of my least favorite phrases. Acknowledging the silver lining is not a bad skill to cultivate in the trivial aftermath of a burnt batch of cookies or a less-than-desirable grade in school. But amid crushing grief and tragic loss, this phrase feels like putting a well-intentioned Band-Aid on a gaping wound. It is crucial to acknowledge the good news that exists even among the bad news, but the good news is not always immediate.

In Genesis 3, we read the first bad news in history and feel the weight of the most significant loss. Adam and Eve are in the Garden of Eden, and everything is complete. Their relationships with God and each other are perfect. Then the serpent deceives the woman and man; they disobey God and receive the curse of sin. The consequences of sin are severe, just, and final. But there is good news.

God declares to the serpent, "I will put hostility between you and the woman, and between your offspring and her offspring. He will strike your head, and you will strike his heel" (Genesis 3:15).

We see reminders that a Savior is coming throughout the Old Testament. Throughout generations, kings, exiles, wars, and famines, the people of Israel expected the Messiah to come while knowing the time may not be near.

As believers today, we have the benefit of hindsight. We can look back to the birth, life, death, and resurrection of Jesus. We can adore the Savior who has come and expect him to come again. Expectation doesn't mute the pain of this world; instead, the pain of this world intensifies our longing for Jesus. We don't need a silver lining; we need to expect the King to come and the Savior to be near us now.

Questions to Ponder

*How has your pain magnified
your longing for Jesus?*

*What truth in Scripture can you
remind yourself of today?*

Scripture Meditation

Isaiah 4:2-6

Freedom

December 2

Introductions never bothered me until I lost a child. "How many kids do you have?" It's a complicated question, and the answer has layers of sadness and even shame. We live in a world that prioritizes labels and categories. If you've ever filed taxes after losing an immediate family member, completed paperwork for an individualized education program, or introduced yourself in a small group at church, you know all too well what boxes you check. It's easy to find our identity in the tags others give us, and some of those classifications sting more than others. Bereaved, single, widowed, sick, divorced, or unemployed carry more weight than a simple descriptor.

In the book of Ruth, we find Naomi, who is both a widow and a bereaved mother. Her labels are the result of an excruciating reality. Understanding the context of her culture and the shame she carried is imperative. To be a widow and lose your sons is horrendous even now, but for Naomi, it left her with nothing except utter grief and disgrace. "'Don't call me Naomi. Call me Mara,' she answered, 'for the Almighty has made me very bitter'" (Ruth 1:20). In her shame and sorrow, Naomi tells people to forgo calling her by her given name, which means "pleasant one," and requests to be called Mara, which means "bitter."

Graciously, Naomi's story doesn't end in bitterness. God provides her family with a relative to act as a redeemer. Once again, Naomi has a child in her lap and hope for the future. God gave Boaz to Ruth, redeeming even Naomi. God gave us Jesus, redeeming even our stories.

Jesus's act of atonement frees us from our sin; it also frees us from the guilt and shame of our circumstances. Jesus offers freedom, and he purchased it with his life. "Child of God," "forgiven," "loved," and "redeemed" won't be boxes to check on our taxes, but they are true nonetheless, and we can hold them close when our sorrow and shame threaten to overwhelm us. We no longer have to be known by our worldly labels; our identity is in Christ.

December 2

Questions to Ponder

*What labels or circumstances bring up
shame or sorrow in your life?*

*How does acknowledging Jesus as your
Redeemer free you and offer you hope?*

Scripture Meditation

1 Peter 2:9-10

7

Our Fears Relieved

December 3

I lost count of how many times I heard the term "freak accident" in the first couple of weeks following my daughter's death. I heard it from doctors, coroners, and family, and I repeated it myself multiple times. While the term aims to bring me comfort, it can also usher in enormous anxiety and fear. Acknowledging that we don't have complete control or know what the future might bring is uncomfortable at best and paralyzing at worst.

Being gifted some of our most significant earthly blessings can also produce some of our most potent fears. When I held my firstborn for the first time, I was astonished by the gift of her life, but I also met anxieties and fears I had never known. My husband is one of the greatest graces in my life, and I tend to worry when he goes for a long run. I think about his route and wonder whether his clothes are bright enough for passing cars to see. Satan often uses the good things in our lives to highlight the possibility of disaster; fear is a tool of the enemy. But living our worst fear can have an unusual effect.

When we have lived the worst, when we have been at our weakest and our fears have been realized, we have the opportunity to experience Jesus profoundly. Living with the pain of loss and uncertainty removes a veil of arrogance that we often let cover Jesus's face. When we acknowledge our fears, we can call them by name and hand them to the one who has overcome the world and reigns victorious over death itself.

Jesus didn't promise us a life free of pain, loss, or suffering, but he did promise us peace. John 16:33 says, "I have told you these things so that in me you may have peace. You will have suffering in this world. Be courageous! I have conquered the world." Our fears may have grown or waned through our circumstances. We may feel brave one day and completely panicked another. But no matter how great our fear, Jesus has come to release us from it. We may not know what tomorrow will bring, but we know the one who holds tomorrow.

Questions to Ponder

What fears and anxieties are enslaving you?

*How does the promise that Christ has
overcome the world give you peace?*

Scripture Meditation

Hebrews 2:14-15

Released from Sin

December 4

It's common to hear someone challenge our faith with the question, "How could a good God allow...." and fill in the blank with tragedy. If we are honest, many of us have also issued that same query in the face of overwhelming difficulty. It doesn't have to be a question of accusation; it can be a question of lament that gives way to worship.

The brokenness and sin of the world are striking. When sin entered the world, the foundation of humanity cracked. Romans tells us that even creation groans in expectation for the returning King. No matter how hard we try to disguise hurt or mask affliction, the truth of our fallenness remains. Understanding the holiness of God and the gravity of sin begins to answer our question of lament. Understanding what we truly deserve and the tremendous gift of grace Jesus offers is of utmost importance.

In Matthew 5, Jesus begins his teaching by extending blessings. At first glance, they seem countercultural, and on further examination, they are genuinely profound. "Blessed are those who mourn, for they will be comforted" (verse 4). Jesus will comfort us in our mourning over tragedy and disappointment; his comfort is the blessing. In this passage, he refers to mourning over our sin. Feeling the weight of our sin and acknowledging our need for a Savior are foundational to finding hope in Jesus. Repentance, not trying to attain perfection, is the way to salvation.

In our grief, it's difficult to wrestle with God's ultimate sovereignty, the sin that so easily entangles, and our perceived innocence. But when we grapple with the truth that all have sinned and fall short of the glory of God, we can't help but worship Jesus, offering him thanks for his mercy and grace. The state of the world and the pain we are enduring magnify our need for Jesus. He came to provide comfort for those that mourn their wickedness, and he alone releases us from the bondage of sin. God's ways may not be our ways, and his thoughts certainly aren't ours, but his way is Jesus, and his gift is eternal life.

December 4

Questions to Ponder

What sin is entangling you?

*Will you repent and allow Jesus to
release you from the bondage of sin?*

Scripture Meditation

Romans 8

Rest for the Weary

December 5

It was 2 a.m., and I sat half-awake in a rocking chair holding my newborn baby. My body was physically tired, and my heart and mind were also thoroughly drained. Welcoming a newborn into our family just five months after losing a child proved to be an incredibly challenging experience. Grief and lack of sleep make a poor team. I was exhausted, I craved respite, but I needed to remember the anointed rest offered by Christ.

When we are physically, emotionally, mentally, and even spiritually tired, our flesh can quickly turn to anger and discouragement. We start wondering, Didn't God promise rest? Where is his rest when grief, loss, or illness ravages our bodies? Wrestling with these questions is good if we allow the Holy Spirit to answer through God's Word.

In Matthew, Jesus beckons, "Come to me, all of you who are weary and burdened, and I will give you rest" (Matthew 11:28). The invitation to take his yoke, for it is easy and light, follows this statement. This bidding seems to be a glorious gift to a weary world, but it isn't until we see Jesus address the Pharisees in the following verses that we understand his true power and offer. Jesus can offer us authentic rest because he is Lord of the Sabbath. Jesus is the Lord of rest.

Often, we don't experience Jesus's ordained rest because we don't want Jesus to be our Lord. We miss Jesus's peace because we expect respite to look like a good night's sleep or the world's promoted self-care routine. John 14:27 says, "Peace I leave with you. My peace I give to you. I do not give to you as the world gives. Don't let your heart be troubled or fearful."

Finding rest in Jesus comes through knowing that he took up our yoke, our burden, and our sin. Jesus came to fulfill the law we cannot satisfy. Christ bore our iniquities and suffered as a perfect sacrifice in our place to offer us eternal rest in him. Jesus has given us peace through the Holy Spirit.

God may bless you with a night of uninterrupted sleep; receive it with thanksgiving. Jesus will often reach us and relieve us from physical exhaustion, but most importantly, he provides us with a peace that passes all understanding, despite our circumstances.

Questions to Ponder

How have you seen Jesus offer you rest physically, emotionally, mentally, and spiritually?

What worldly rest do you desires in place of true rest from Jesus?

Scripture Meditation

Matthew 11:28-12:8

Strength in Weakness

December 6

Unfortunately, the current measurement of someone's strength and ability is found somewhere in the statement, "How do they do it all?" Our standard of achievement has become quantitative based on how much we can calmly and gracefully accomplish without breaking a sweat. Receiving bad news can be one of the most weakening moments in life. A poor health diagnosis, a loss of job or security, a betrayal, or a death of a loved one can strip us bare and sap us of any strength we had. And yet, our response to these life-altering moments is often measured by how well we are "handling it."

Strength is often spoken of and demonstrated in the Bible; true strength is in the hand of the Almighty. The current culture contorts this God-ordained, Jesus-empowered, and Holy Spirit–given strength. Philippians 4:13 has become a popular mantra for winning the big game or getting the next job promotion. Except Paul penned his words to the Philippians from prison and had learned to be content in all circumstances. His message was that we could accomplish the will of God through the power of Jesus no matter the situation, not necessarily ace the upcoming final.

Paul speaks again of the power of strength found through Christ in 2 Corinthians. His power is made perfect in my weakness. Power through weakness is a countercultural notion because we misunderstand genuine strength and underestimate the power of Jesus.

Strength is not checking everything off the to-do list with hours to spare. It isn't holding in our emotions and putting on a brave front. The power of Jesus being made perfect in our weakness is often the ability to offer thanksgiving to a holy God amid crushing grief. Sometimes strength is weeping openly with faint prayers on our lips. The world around us may scoff and say that these things are inadequate and powerless. But when we have been made weak, we realize we can only receive strength from the one who, in pain and anguish, prayed, "Not my will, but yours, be done" (Luke 22:42).

When circumstances and hardships deprive us of our perceived power, we need only look to the Savior for supernatural strength. As we stop relying on self-sufficiency, we begin to behold the true strength of Jesus and see how he carries us graciously forward.

Questions to Ponder

*What circumstances and difficulties
have rendered you weak?*

*How do you see Christ's power
displayed in your weakness?*

Scripture Meditation

2 Corinthians 12:6-10

Consolation

December 7

Since my daughter's passing, I have been offered many condolences, received cards in the hundreds, and accepted numerous thoughtful gifts. It is a beautiful testament to the incredible friends and family we have all over the world. To see the body of Christ be the hands and feet of Jesus in tangible ways is an offering of comfort I won't soon forget.

Amid the notes and tokens of encouragement, several offered more significant comfort. Mothers who had also lost a child, wives that had buried their husbands, and siblings who had parted with a brother or sister too soon were able to offer unique comfort that others couldn't.

Most of us on a road of suffering would not wish the same pain on anyone else. We don't desire others to know the sting of death, the bitterness of betrayal, or the misery of dreams shattered. At the same time, we are grateful for those who have gone before us, the ones who have embarked on a similar journey and are farther up the road. We soak in their comfort and support.

To be known and feel understood is a powerful tool of comfort. We can more easily receive encouragement from those we believe may comprehend our circumstances. Jesus gives us this true and knowing comfort, and he offers it for a reason.

Paul writes to the Corinthians, saying, "For just as the sufferings of Christ overflow to us, so also through Christ our comfort overflows" (2 Corinthians 1:5). Christ humbled himself to the point of death on a cross. He knows pain intimately, and he knows the suffering you must endure on this side of eternity. Christ also grants us the comfort he received from the Father and the Holy Spirit, and he desires for us to give it to others.

Suffering can be lonely, and it often feels that no one can console us because no one can understand what we are going through. But Jesus understands, and his consolation is so abundant that it overflows. He will send people into our lives to comfort us, and one day he will send us to others to comfort them.

Questions to Ponder

*Who has been an instrument
of godly comfort in your life?*

*How do you see the consolation
of Jesus overflow into your life?*

Scripture Meditation

2 Corinthians 1:3-11

Sure Hope

December 8

Part of the grieving process is coming to terms with all of the things you are grieving. I mourn the loss of my daughter and what was, but I also suffer the loss of what might have been. I had hopes and dreams for my daughter that I didn't even realize I had until they were all stripped away. I won't teach her to tie her shoes, take her to kindergarten, or see her learn to read. There will be no graduation, no wedding, and no grandchildren. These are secondary losses, but the sting of hope unrealized is still powerful.

As a society, our words carry less weight because we use more words without considering their meaning. The definition of *hope* has changed with time. Merriam-Webster defines *hope* as cherishing a desire with anticipation, to want something to happen or be true. The same dictionary notes that the archaic meaning of hope is to expect with confidence, to trust.

What I wanted for my daughter was the first definition of hope. It was wishful; I desired an uncertain outcome. The hope I have in Jesus is the biblical and archaic definition: it is a firm trust.

Hebrews 6:19-20 says, "We have this hope as an anchor for the soul, firm and secure. It enters the inner sanctuary behind the curtain. Jesus has entered there on our behalf as a forerunner, because he has become a high priest forever according to the order of Melchizedek."

Jesus is the anchor of our hope. The promises found in the work of Christ are sure and secure. The hope we have in Jesus will not disappoint or put us to shame. Though our motives should center on seeing the glory of God, it isn't wrong to have dreams and desires for the future. But we must learn to hold transient uncertainties loosely. We have all been disappointed, and we know the pain of lamenting losses. Our hope in Jesus is not wishful because Jesus will not fail. In a world full of sorrow and dashed dreams, hold firmly to the one who anchors our souls. Find sure hope in the Rock of Ages.

Questions to Ponder

What desires and dreams have you lost?

*How do the certainty and firm hope
of Jesus Christ encourage you?*

Scripture Meditation

Romans 5:1-5

Dear Desire

December 9

As a young girl, I knew I wanted to get married and have children one day. I prayed for my future husband, and I prayed for future children. Sometimes the prayers were notably selfish, but sometimes they were so pure as I sought God's will. Now, married and a mother, I still pray for my husband and my children. I have prayed for my children to know the Lord as their Savior for years. In fact, with every positive pregnancy test I've held in my hand, my first prayer has been more like thought whispered through a breath, "Thank you for this baby; please let them know you."

When my daughter unexpectedly passed away, I began wrestling with my desires. In the immediacy of the tragedy, shock left me stripped down to foundational faith and truth. God is good. God is sovereign. He holds all things together. As the shock started to fade, the actual wrestling began. How was this tragedy good? Is it wrong that I wanted to raise my daughter and see her grow to live a long life? What are the true desires of my heart? It took time and prayer to see that God works all things together for the good of those who love him. I see the answered prayer for my daughter; she now knows the Lord better than I can imagine, even if not in the way I expected.

Psalm 37:4 says, "Take delight in the Lord, and he will give you your heart's desires."

In an affluent world, it's easy to mistake our desires. Health and wealth usually climb to the top of the list, salvation gets an honorable mention, and delighting in the Lord comes in last place. But when we have had the metaphorical rug ripped from beneath our feet, we start to see the desires of our hearts resemble the desires of our Father's heart. We have no room for superficial nuances, and we desire Jesus so much it causes an ache deep within.

Jesus is the answer to our wrestling. Jesus sits with us in our sorrows and meets us when our faith is only foundational facts. Jesus is the desire of every heart, whether they know it or not.

Questions to Ponder

How have you seen Jesus meet your desires?

What desires has God removed from your heart?

Scripture Meditation

Psalm 84

Every Nation

December 10

A profound loss gives us a unique vantage point to see our own lives and the world differently. Suffering makes us confront our beliefs head-on and peel back layers of wrong ideology. Am I a follower of Christ purely to receive blessings? Am I willing to take up my cross daily? Is what I consider beneficial what God deems profitable?

Too often, we find that we have meddled wrongly with the narrative of Scripture. We can start to believe that God is for us and our agendas instead of seeing that we are part of His design. When we tamper with the gospel and westernize it, we strip the good news of its power. If it isn't good news to all people, it isn't the gospel of Jesus Christ. Perhaps the Lord may bless us with good health, numerous material provisions, safety, and security, but that isn't guaranteed.

In Joshua 2, we read the story of Rahab. She is a prostitute and foreigner, but even she knows the power of the God of the Israelites. When she welcomes two Israelite spies into her house, she confesses that she knows the Lord will have her land and that terror has fallen on her and the surrounding city. We see clearly that the presence of God is decisive, bringing courage to those who are with him and terror to those against him. Rahab pleads to be shown compassion in return for her kindness to Israel.

God does show Rahab kindness. Not only is she spared, but she gets to be a part of God's salvation plan. The next time the Bible mentions Rahab is in the genealogy of Jesus. Rahab becomes a beautiful picture of the promise given to Abraham: "All the nations of the earth will be blessed by your offspring" (Genesis 22:18). Jesus is the ultimate fulfillment of that promise, and we can see throughout Scripture how God brought many others into his family.

The good news of the gospel is redemption through the blood of Jesus Christ. It may not give you earthly wealth, you may be physically sick for the rest of this life, and you may lose everything precious to you, but God is the God of redemption, and that good news is available for you and every other person in this world.

Questions to Ponder

What hardships have caused you to take a deeper look at the truth of the gospel?

How does knowing that God offers redemption through his Son provide encouragement amid suffering?

Scripture Meditation

Revelation 7:9-12

Joy

December 11

A Sunday roast was in the center of the table, my friends and family filled the seats, and laughter was a welcome guest. It was a typical day for my family; we were content and happy. The very next day, my home was filled with people, but happiness was unmistakably absent. The shock and tragedy of my daughter's death hung heavily. In just twenty-four hours, our circumstances were a far cry from the warmth felt around our dining table the day before. It was baffling, and I wondered if happiness would ever be a fixture in our home again. In a broken and painful world where our circumstances can change on a dime, joy can seem elusive or fluctuate at a nauseating pace.

Happiness and joy are not exactly the same. While happiness can seem elusive, the Lord assures us of true joy found in him. Jesus tells us plainly how our joy may be complete in John 15:9-11, "As the Father has loved me, I have also loved you. Remain in my love. If you keep my commands you will remain in my love, just as I have kept my Father's commands and remain in his love. I have told you these things so that my joy may be in you and your joy may be complete."

This is a beautiful promise. Interestingly, it comes right before he warns us of persecution. When Jesus offered us the hope of complete joy, he wasn't offering comfort and a worldly view of happiness. He was assuring us of perfect joy found in his presence, even amid the hurt and suffering of this world.

As time passes, we learn that joy and grief are not exclusive. The two frequently work together in a perplexing harmony. The greater our joy, the more the pain of this life becomes evident. The more our grief grows, the more we are offered clarity, and our joy in the Lord will abound. Happiness will come and go, but the joy of the Lord is steadfast.

Questions to Ponder

*What examples in your own life can you find of
temporal happiness and the true joy of Jesus?*

*How have you seen the joy of the Lord
magnified in the pain of your circumstances?*

Scripture Meditation

Psalm 16

Longing Heart

December 12

Children are the greatest source of questions. Their appetite for learning and discovery surpasses most adults. How, what, when, and why rank at the top of a child's vocabulary, and we should learn from their example. Even amid disappointment and frustration, a child who may not be self-aware of their emotions will still be able to muster questions. Somewhere between adolescence and adulthood, we stop asking as many questions. This trend can pour over into our relationship with God too.

Perhaps asking questions of God seems faithless, or maybe it feels disrespectful of his holiness. As Christians, we have neglected lament and longing. Lament is a prayerful response to pain that leads to trust. Lament is a biblical and powerful way of presenting our questions to God.

Psalm 139:1-2 tells us, "Lord, you have searched me and known me. You know when I sit down and when I stand up; you understand my thoughts from far away."

There is no reason to mask or subdue our honest questions before the Lord because he already knows our hearts and thoughts. Longing expressed through biblical lament allows us to wrestle with the pain of our circumstances while trusting in the promises of God. Longing is a need met only in the fullness of Jesus.

Hebrews 4:15-16 says, "For we do not have a high priest who is unable to sympathize with our weaknesses, but one who has been tempted in every way as we are, yet without sin. Therefore, let us approach the throne of grace with boldness, so that we may receive mercy and find grace to help us in time of need."

Even when we are weak, we can ask boldly. Loss, grief, and disappointment have a way of stripping away pretense and calibrating the longing of our hearts. No longer are the questions of our hearts petty and insignificant; they are profound. We can ask the deep questions of God because he holds all understanding. As we lament before the Lord, we will find some questions answered. But we will also find that God becomes our focus amid lingering questions. No matter the questions and longing of our hearts, they can all be answered in Christ.

Questions to Ponder

What questions have you withheld from God?

How are you encouraged to lament, knowing that Jesus sympathizes with you and mediates for you?

Scripture Meditation

Psalm 13

Deliverer

December 13

For three weeks following my daughter's death, I always had at least one person (and often several people) in my home to help. People were bringing meals, doing laundry, or playing with my children. Then suddenly, our world went into quarantine. Social distancing tore away the privilege of community inside our home and the offers of tangible help. Ordinary tasks felt overwhelming. It was as if I was moving through a fog of grief and everything I tried to do was in slow motion. I was frustrated, and self-pity began to creep into my heart.

We should not view grief negatively in our lives. It is normal and healthy to grieve when we have experienced loss, sorrow, and disappointment. Grief is a demonstration of love. On the other hand, self-pity is a demonstration of pride. Jesus will comfort us in our grief, but he seeks to deliver us from the snare of pride.

The exodus is the example of deliverance we most often think of, but God delivers his people throughout Scripture. It wasn't an easy journey when the Israelites left Egypt. The act of deliverance is often a painful process. But the Lord does not leave things incomplete; we can't mistake our pain as his inactivity. When God acts as Rescuer and Redeemer, he delivers us from something and into something else.

Psalm 40:2-3 says, "He brought me up from a desolate pit, out of the muddy clay, and set my feet on a rock, making my steps secure. He put a new song in my mouth, a hymn of praise to our God. Many will see and fear, and they will trust in the Lord."

Jesus has delivered us from sin and death into abundant and eternal life with him. God desires to deliver us from the oppression of sin. Grief may be heavy, but it isn't fundamentally sin. In the hands of Jesus, grief will become lighter and produce sanctification. But pain in the enemy's hands can bring an onslaught of temptation with self-pity ranking at the top. Jesus desires to meet us in our suffering. It is Jesus who can take us out of the slimy pit of despair and put a new song in our mouths. Jesus is our deliverer.

Questions to Ponder

*What sin has ensnared you as you
face disappointment and grief?*

*What new song of praise has Jesus
given you through deliverance?*

Scripture Meditation

Psalm 40

Humility in Life and Death

December 14

I have had the opportunity and joy of holding all of my babies immediately after giving birth. Their delicate bodies were placed directly on my chest, as I cradled their helpless warmth against myself. It is a blessing and honor I won't soon forget. Unfortunately, I have also had the horrific experience of holding my daughter's lifeless body in my arms. Her frame was once again entirely helpless, and I carried her in shock and distress.

We tend to think of the humility of Jesus in his suffering and death alone. We don't often spend time meditating on the humility he displayed just by being human. The beginnings and endings of life are the most vulnerable. This does not render Jesus weak but humble.

The arc of Jesus's life on earth is framed in humility. We see the beginning of his life early in the book of Luke: "Then she gave birth to her firstborn son, and she wrapped him tightly in cloth and laid him in a manger, because there was no guest room available" (Luke 2:7). Many chapters later, we read about his death: "He [Joseph of Arimathea] approached Pilate and asked for Jesus's body. Taking it down, he wrapped it in fine linen and placed it in a tomb cut into the rock, where no one had ever been placed" (Luke 23:52-53).

He was born into the world in humility, as a babe having to be wrapped in cloth by another and placed in a manger. He left the world in humility, enduring the cross, his corpse being wrapped in cloth by another and placed in a tomb.

The very nature of human life should humble us. The example that Christ willingly displayed should humble us. Many of us have lived through moments and circumstances in life that have stripped us bare of our hopes, dreams, and securities. We need to let those moments humble us, not destroy us. Jesus's work of atonement for our sin should create bold confidence in who he is and propel us to rely on him. Our humility is not a sign of weakness; it is a sign of faithful surrender.

Questions to Ponder

What events in your life have humbled you?

*How does Jesus's example of humility encourage
you to walk in faithful submission to God's plans?*

Scripture Meditation

Philippians 2:1-8

Yet a King

December 15

"Jesus, please be near." It's a prayer that has echoed from my lips numerous times since losing a child. I need Jesus, the Prince of Peace, to meet me in the quiet and lonely places. I need his rest to fall on the loud and abrasive moments. Jesus is many things, including our Prince of Peace, but he is also the King. Amid significant loss and sorrow, we tend to gravitate to Jesus, our comfort and peace, but we should not overlook his kingship.

Most of us live in a democracy, and our voice has the power of choice. It is a privilege and an honor. Because we don't live in a time or a country where a king holds supreme power, we can tend to downplay the significance of Jesus as King.

In John, we see a Gentile and unbeliever recognize Jesus as King. John 18:37 says, "'You are a king then?' Pilate asked. 'You say that I'm a king,' Jesus replied. 'I was born for this, and I have come into this world for this: to testify to the truth. Everyone who is of the truth listens to my voice.'" Later in chapter 19, Pilate defends his choice to write "King of the Jews" on the sign on the cross, saying, "What I have written, I have written." Jesus wasn't making an empty claim; he was proclaiming the truth of his reign.

Jesus is the rightful King, and he declares himself as such. The prophecies Jesus fulfilled point to his proper place as King. After the first coming of Jesus as King, we can still choose to follow him, and forgiveness is offered. We can willingly submit to him and serve him, or we can reject him and despise him. There is no neutral ground. When Jesus returns once more, his kingship will leave no room for choice. Philippians 2:10-11 says, "At the name of Jesus every knee will bow—in heaven and on earth and under the earth—and every tongue will confess that Jesus Christ is Lord, to the glory of God the Father."

Jesus is holy; therefore, he is a perfect king. He is just and gracious; he is powerful and kind. He is the King of might that came gentle and lowly, riding on a donkey. This King is the same Savior who meets us in our suffering and turns our mourning into dancing. He is a King worthy of our adoration.

Questions to Ponder

*Do you tend to gravitate toward specific names
or attributes of Jesus? If so, which ones?*

*How does Christ's kingship today and in
his second coming encourage you?*

Scripture Meditation
Psalm 47

Reign in Us

December 16

It was Christmas Eve, and our four children were opening their traditional gift of Christmas pajamas before heading off to bed. Our youngest daughter, just two and a half, noticed an extra gift bag. When the kids discovered that the gift was for all of them, they quickly unwrapped the present to find an ultrasound picture. There was an eruption of joy when they realized that they would be welcoming a new sibling in the coming year. It is still one of our favorite stories and memories.

Just two months later, my husband called the OB-GYN office. "I'm sorry, we need to reschedule my wife's ultrasound for the anatomy scan. Our two-year-old," the words caught in his chest, "passed away last night." Our life had done a complete turnaround. We went from abounding joy to overwhelming sorrow. Our life that had been full of comfort and ease now was painful and disorienting.

It is easy to praise a sovereign God when things are going well. But as soon as we perceive that things are not going according to our plan, or life becomes painful, we quickly point fingers at the one in charge or ignore him completely.

We aren't the first to be tempted to reject Jesus's sovereign reign. Matthew 21 tells us that the chief priests and elders of the people went to Jesus and challenged him, asking, "Who gave you this authority?" (verse 23). The Jewish people wanted a king. They were looking forward to someone coming and saving them, but when the King arrived and didn't do things the way they wanted, they pointed fingers, plotted against him, and ultimately rejected him.

If Jesus asked us if we would like to begin down a road of suffering, most of us would say no, if we were honest. Providentially, Jesus doesn't ask our permission, but in his grace and mercy, he allows us to submit willingly to his sovereign plan. Jesus has much to teach us through pleasure and abundance, but he will shape us through adversity and pain. We may easily let God reign over our joy and comfort, but will we let him reign over our suffering too?

Questions to Ponder

*In what ways have you wrestled with
God's reign and sovereignty?*

*How can you trust Jesus with your
suffering and pain today?*

Scripture Meditation

Colossians 1:15-23

Eternity in Our Hearts

December 17

When we live through a traumatic event, lose someone dear to us, or experience the sobering grief of the world around us, our perception of time can be entangled with hope and dread. We long to be with Jesus. The idea that we might have many more years to wait on this broken earth before seeing our Savior or a loved one gone often feels cruel. We want time to speed up. Yet, we also see the beautiful things in our lives now and a clear call from Scripture that there is work to do here. The more time marches on, the closer we are to heaven, yet the further we are from fond memories, and we may still have more earthly pain to endure.

Wrestling with the effects of time can be made even more challenging during the nostalgia of Christmas and the newness of an upcoming year. Ecclesiastes 3:11 meets us with a beautiful reminder. God has made everything appropriate in its time, and he has also put eternity in our hearts. When time confounds us, hope seems too far to touch, and new beginnings feel like a betrayal, it is a comfort to know who holds time and that he has a purpose.

Just before Jesus was betrayed, arrested, and ultimately murdered as an innocent man, he prayed, "Father, the hour has come. Glorify your Son so that the Son may glorify you, since you gave him authority over all people, so that he may give eternal life to everyone you have given him. *This is eternal life: that they may know you, the only true God, and the one you have sent—Jesus Christ*" (John 17:1-3, emphasis mine).

Knowing Jesus is experiencing eternal life, and that doesn't have to wait for our last breath. Time might feel harsh, and the holidays may bring baffling emotions, but remember, we are sojourners, and this world is not our forever home. Fix your eyes on Jesus, press on faithfully, and relish the eternity he has placed in your heart. One day all really will be made new.

Questions to Ponder

How has time felt burdensome or perplexing?

*How does the truth that God has put
eternity in our hearts encourage you?*

Scripture Meditation

Ecclesiastes 3:1-15

Gracious

December 18

James 1:17 says, "Every good and perfect gift is from above, coming down from the Father of lights, who does not change like shifting shadows." It's a verse spoken often in our home, one of the first Bible verses my kids learn, and it is etched at the base of my daughter's headstone. She was a good gift, and the Lord gave her to us.

It's humbling to sit and meditate on the good gifts God has given. *Mercy*, by definition, means sparing us of what we do deserve, while *grace*, by definition, means giving us what we don't deserve. Some good gifts of grace and mercy from the Lord are more evident than others: family, health, and provisions. But do we look for and recognize all of his grace and goodness even in suffering?

Romans 8 tells us that God works all things for the good of those who love him and are called according to his purpose. This truth can be hard to reconcile in the aftermath of devastating circumstances, and it is usually because our definition of *good* is different from God's.

Neglecting the book of Job is typical until you have lived your own worst nightmares, then it becomes a treasure and a mentor. After Job experiences his first wave of devastating tragedy, he famously says, "The Lord gives, and the Lord takes away. Blessed be the name of the Lord" (Job 1:21). Job recognizes that it is the giver we should praise, not the gift. God answers Job's lament and wrestling at the end of the book. God restores Job's fortunes and doubles his previous possessions. It's tempting to see these material blessings as the only abundant grace God offers. However, in Job 42:5 when Job replies, "I had heard reports about you [God], but now my eyes have seen you," we see the most excellent measure of grace: the gift of knowing God.

The grace God offers is his Son, Jesus. God's good is the gift of salvation, and it is the most extraordinary grace we could ever imagine. We see that we should praise the giver, God, and the given, Jesus.

God intends to demonstrate his glory through us; even our suffering can display his majesty. Through grief and sorrow, we have a unique opportunity to know God more intimately because of the atoning work of Jesus. To know Jesus more is always a good gift from the Father.

Questions to Ponder

What are good gifts in your life from the Father?

*How have you come to know
Jesus more through suffering?*

Scripture Meditation

James 1:2-18

Kingdom Bring

December 19

Losing someone dear to us, seeing our plans change drastically, or even growing older puts in sharp focus the brevity of life on this earth. Living today in light of eternity is our calling, yet dwelling on the in-between is where we spend most of our energy. It's our greatest time waster and one of Satan's most potent tools against us. Fear, anxiety, apathy, and general selfishness tend to steal our focus. Instead of focusing on the moment God has given us, we think about the times and days that are not guaranteed.

James warns us that we make plans about the future, yet we don't even know what tomorrow will bring: "You are like vapor that appears for a little while, then vanishes" (James 4:14).

While we don't know what tomorrow will bring, we know what God has planned for eternity. Daniel 4:3 says, "His kingdom is an eternal kingdom, and his dominion is from generation to generation."

The Lord's Prayer is often one of the first Scripture passages we learn as children; we recite it and say it often. "Our Father in heaven, your name be honored as holy. Your kingdom come. Your will be done on earth as it is in heaven. Give us today our daily bread. And forgive us our debts, as we also have forgiven our debtors. And do not bring us into temptation, but deliver us from the evil one" (Matthew 6:9-13).

Jesus is not only teaching us how to pray, he is also teaching us how to live. Trust the Lord to meet your daily needs without worrying about tomorrow's demands. Forgive, as we are forgiven. We should pray for God's kingdom to come and his will to be done; we should also live that way.

One day God's kingdom will be manifest on earth, and Jesus Christ will rule. Most of us truly long for that day, and we eagerly wait for a day when Jesus will wipe away every tear. We can live with purpose today, knowing God's kingdom is everlasting. Jesus will meet our needs today, and if he gives us tomorrow, he will meet us there too. Jesus alone can provide us with patience as we wait and purpose as we live.

December 19

Questions to Ponder

*In what ways are you tempted to get
distracted with the "in-between" days?*

*How do your life and prayers show your
desire for the coming of God's kingdom?*

Scripture Meditation

Psalm 90

75

Eternal Spirit

December 20

I sat in a dining room chair and watched people bustle around the room. I was in shock. Paramedics had just taken my fourth child to a hospital where soon she would be pronounced dead. My house was full of people. Numerous paramedics, countless sheriff's department troopers, and a neighbor who was helping my surviving children out the door. People surrounded me, yet I felt utterly alone. Even though I was experiencing shock, it wouldn't be the last time I felt alone in a crowd of people.

Thanksgiving dinners, Christmas festivities, a child's talent show or sporting event, family get-togethers, and even church became places of loneliness amid crowds of people. It's a perplexing sentiment unless you have experienced it yourself. Suffering is lonely, and loneliness is one of the most crushing positions. Whether we have been left, been betrayed, or experienced loss, the reality of feeling abandoned and isolated is paramount, yet for those in Christ, we are never truly alone.

In John 16, Jesus is speaking with his disciples, explaining that the time is soon coming when he must leave them. Jesus goes on to say, "It is for your benefit that I go away, because if I don't go away the Counselor will not come to you. If I go, I will send him to you" (verse 7). These are his friends, his followers, and they are confused and sorrowful. How can Jesus leaving them be a good thing? His answer is the Counselor, the Eternal Spirit.

God gave us the gift of His Son, Jesus, who then gave us the gift of the Holy Spirit. As followers of Christ, we have the indwelling of his Eternal Spirit. We are never alone.

As Paul writes, "For you did not receive a spirit of slavery to fall back into fear. Instead, you received the Spirit of adoption, by whom we cry out, 'Abba, Father!' The Spirit himself testifies together with our spirit that we are God's children, and if children, also heirs—heirs of God and coheirs with Christ—if indeed we suffer with him so that we may also be glorified with him" (Romans 8:15-17).

Suffering may seem to isolate us from the people around us, but it draws us closer to Jesus by his Spirit. The eternal promise of the nearness of Jesus is one of the greatest gifts to a lonely world.

Questions to Ponder

*When have you experienced
loneliness or isolation this year?*

*How does the promise of the
Holy Spirit encourage you?*

Scripture Meditation

Psalm 139:7-12

Ruler

December 21

"It's not fair!" It was a phrase that I forbid in our home one January morning. I was tired of hearing that someone's breakfast serving was larger or someone else had less homework. We needed to be content, not complain. But just a few weeks later, I sat on my porch feeling like life wasn't fair. There were three children, not four, playing in the front yard. My thoughts wandered to the story of Abraham and Isaac. I felt my flesh rise and say, "But you provided a ram for Abraham!" Instantly, the Lord replied, "I provided a Lamb for you; his name is Jesus." I repented.

Typically, we gravitate to God's love and grace, and it isn't wrong to worship and appreciate his lovingkindness. But we can't overlook that God is a just ruler, especially when things feel unfair.

Many of us know the effects of a broken and sinful world, perhaps through malice, betrayal, or abandonment. What is God's just response? Romans 12:19 says, "Friends, do not avenge yourselves; instead, leave room for God's wrath, because it is written, Vengeance belongs to me; I will repay, says the Lord." God is holy, and while it might seem delayed, his justice and timing are perfect.

For many, our sorrow and tragedy are not a direct result of sin. These situations leave us overwhelmed and perplexed. Why did this happen? Why me? Why us? Why them? They are questions of lament, and God will answer them with grace and justice. In the book of Job, we see at least twenty chapters of Job's lament. God's response is a thunderous clap of justice. Between Job 38 and 41, God declares his just rule. We see the perfect display of grace and righteousness.

Job's story seems insignificant compared to the most unfair event in history, when the spotless Lamb of God hung on a cross for our sins. Yet, through God's perfect justice and grace, Jesus is our salvation. Because of Jesus's work of atonement, God demonstrates his justice by forgiving us. As 1 John 1:9 tells us, "If we confess our sins, he is faithful and righteous to forgive us our sins and to cleanse us from all unrighteousness." God holds the scales of justice, and he weighs them perfectly. In our wrestling and lament, we must trust the one who rules with justice. We must trust the Lamb provided for us.

Questions to Ponder

*In what ways have you felt your
circumstances were unfair?*

*How can you trust God with your questions and
pain today, knowing he rules with justice?*

Scripture Meditation

Isaiah 11:1-10

Sufficient Merit

December 22

Some of the most overwhelming moments early in my grief came when I felt the weight of my grief paired with my children's grief. Carrying sorrow is heavy, but navigating the journey while holding multiple little hearts often left me beyond my means. I couldn't move forward each day; I was unable to carry all of the broken pieces of our hearts.

Many things in life deplete us and leave us feeling inadequate, and as we are finite humans, this is not uncommon or even wrong. We were never meant to do it all, accomplish everything, or be entirely self-sufficient. We are meant to rely on Jesus, and he is enough. But do we believe that?

In John 14, Philip makes a request:

> "Lord," said Philip, "show us the Father, and that's enough for us." Jesus said to him, "Have I been among you all this time and you do not know me, Philip? The one who has seen me has seen the Father. How can you say, 'Show us the Father'? Don't you believe that I am in the Father and the Father is in me? The words I speak to you I do not speak on my own. The Father who lives in me does his works. Believe

> me that I am in the Father and the Father is in me. Otherwise, believe because of the works themselves." John 14:8-11

If we aren't careful, we can live like Philip, wanting another sign, a special revelation, or something else. But Jesus has clearly displayed his sufficiency, and he is asking us to trust him. Like Philip, we need to remember that Jesus is sufficient; Jesus is enough.

We cannot add anything to the Lord. Having faith in Christ means trusting in his sufficiency. In our need, Jesus is enough to provide for us. In our weakness, Jesus is enough to strengthen us. Jesus is enough to equip, bless, and guide us. And most importantly, while we were still sinners, Jesus was enough to save us.

Questions to Ponder

*What circumstances have made you
feel helpless and inadequate?*

*How does the knowledge that Jesus is
sufficient encourage you today?*

Scripture Meditation

Hebrews 1:1-4

Raise Us

December 23

Reading great literature and watching well-made films are some of my favorite pastimes. At the heart of my enjoyment is the love of a great story. The most famous and beloved stories in history involve sorrow and often death, and it is these moments of grief that illuminate joy and purpose. The most extraordinary story of all time is no different. Jesus's life, death, and resurrection was not a backup plan; it was always a part of the story.

Timothy writes, "He has saved us and called us with a holy calling, not according to our works, but according to his own purpose and grace, which was given to us in Christ Jesus before time began" (2 Timothy 1:9). As believers, we rightfully celebrate the resurrection of Jesus; it is the hope of the gospel to raise us to new life. Yet, we often don't meditate on and mourn what had to come first. There must be a death to have a resurrection.

Our very nature wants to live forever, and it isn't a wrong desire; it is God-given as God created us with eternity in our hearts. Of course, we have corrupted this notion far beyond living a healthy and purposeful life—often we will do everything in our power to live a life of comfort on this earth for as long as possible. The reverse is true too. God is the creator of life, and we cannot be quick to take it; he alone ordains our days.

When we repent of our sins, trust in Jesus, and confess him as Lord of our lives, we die to ourselves. Galatians tells us that we have been crucified with Christ, and it is no longer we who live, but Christ who lives in us (Galatians 2:20). We celebrate that we are new creations—the old has gone, and the new has come.

One day there will be another resurrection. As 1 Thessalonians 4:16 tells us, "For the Lord himself will descend from heaven with a shout, with the archangel's voice, and with the trumpet of God, and the dead in Christ will rise first."

When we have felt the sting of death, understand the weight of sin, and mourn the pain of this world, we can't help but worship the living God. Death is the fate we will all face, but because of Jesus, it isn't the end of the story.

Questions to Ponder

*How has your understanding of death
magnified your worship of Jesus?*

What hope do you find in being raised to new life?

Scripture Meditation

1 Corinthians 15:20-28

Glorious Throne

December 24

Christmas draws our attention to the incarnation of Jesus. We meditate on his life as a baby, how he grew in wisdom and stature, and his earthly ministry. Jesus is fully God and fully man. The story continues, and our worship grows. Jesus is the way, the truth, and the life. Jesus bought our salvation with his life, and he has the scars to prove it.

A beautiful verse in the popular Christmas hymn "Away in a Manger" says, "Fit us for heaven to live with thee there." What does it mean to be fit for heaven? How is God preparing us to live with him there? The answer is in our justification through the atoning work of Jesus and our sanctification through the ongoing work of the Holy Spirit (Hebrews 10:10; Philippians 1:6). One day this will lead to our glorification (Colossians 3:4).

Jesus justified us with his life. In the gospel of John, we see Jesus resurrected and with his disciples. Thomas is famous for his doubt, but thanks to his story, we glimpse the significance of Jesus's scars. John 20:27-28 says, "Then he [Jesus] said to Thomas, 'Put your finger here and look at my hands. Reach out your hand and put it into my side. Don't be faithless, but believe.' Thomas responded to him, 'My Lord and my God!'"

Jesus's scars were not in vain; neither are ours. Often, our sanctification comes through immense suffering in this life. We are frequently fit for heaven by loss, heartache, and sorrow. Our scars tether us to our need for Jesus, and our pain renders the things of this world dim. Scars are a testament to wounds, but they also speak of healing. Jesus still bears his scars, and I hope we will too. One day we will appear in glory with Jesus, and our life on this earth will be the prologue to a magnificent and never-ending story.

Questions to Ponder

How do you see Jesus fitting you for heaven through suffering?

In what ways does the promise of eternity with Jesus encourage you?

Scripture Meditation

Revelation 5

Conclusion

One day after visiting my daughter's grave on Thanksgiving, I found myself alone with my Bible in my lap. It was early in the morning, and the sting of death felt especially severe. My eyes closed tight as I whispered, "Come, Lord Jesus. Please." The melody of a familiar song filled my mind, and the pain of loss ebbed ever so slightly.

Come, Thou long expected Jesus
Born to set Thy people free;
From our fears and sins release us,
Let us find our rest in Thee.
Israel's strength and consolation,
Hope of all the earth Thou art;
Dear desire of every nation,
Joy of every longing heart.
Born Thy people to deliver,
Born a child and yet a King,
Born to reign in us forever,
Now Thy gracious kingdom bring.
By Thine own eternal Spirit
Rule in all our hearts alone;
By Thine all sufficient merit,
Raise us to Thy glorious throne.

Charles Wesley penned the words to this beloved Advent hymn in 1744. At the time, he lived in a city with rampant sin, weak religion, immense poverty, countless orphans, and indifference to those suffering. He witnessed a weary world, and he knew Christ came for those hurting. Charles Wesley expressed his desire for Christ to come again and make all things new.

"Come, Thou Long Expected Jesus" had always been one of my favorite hymns, but now it was the groaning of my heart put to song. In a season when I couldn't quite get myself to utter the words "Merry Christmas," I could earnestly plead, "Now Thy gracious kingdom bring." This hymn was never far from my mind the first Christmas season after my daughter passed, and one day it became the framework for the Advent you've just read.

If this Christmas season has felt heavy to you, too, I'm so sorry. If grief, pain, and disappointment seem more familiar than cheer, you aren't alone. If you are weary, remember, Jesus came for you. Christmas is a reminder that Christ has come, and while we live in a world full of pain, we hold on to the truth that Christ will come again.

This Christmas, I'm praying for you. While things might not seem merry and bright, it's possible to celebrate Jesus with tear-filled eyes. We can hold gratitude for the gift of salvation because we acknowledge the pain of this world. Jesus is near us now, and we expect him to come again.

Acknowledgements

When pain enters our story, it can often produce bitterness and ungratefulness. Fortunately, suffering also can pave the way for tremendous gratitude. While I've had many moments of anger and discontentment, by the grace of Jesus, I've experienced far more thanksgiving.

It's God who has ordained my days and my story. Even amid great hurt, I'm grateful to see his sovereign hand weave the threads of providence and grace. His grace is sufficient, and his ways are not my own. I have received incredible comfort from the Father, and I'm grateful that he has allowed me to offer comfort to others (2 Corinthians 1:4).

Robert, when it comes to writing, you're my biggest advocate and my greatest encouragement. Without your unwavering faith in this book, it would have never come to fruition. I mean it when I say that you're my favorite person in every arena of life.

For my kids here, you've given me one of the most significant roles in my life. I appreciate your patience as writing began joining my full-time job as your mommy.

To my sweet daughter already there, what a joy to be your mommy. You still inspire me every day, and I can't wait for the day when I'll see you again.

I have had incredible support from friends, family, and sweet writing communities. Brooke, Mackenzie, Jeff, Kelli, Mark, Julie, Martha, Sandy, the Songs in the Night community, Hope Family Care friends, the team at Yates and Yates, and many more. You have prayed, encouraged, and read early drafts; thank you.

Kristen Defevers and Mike Fontecchio, thank you for making this book consistently beautiful. It was a pleasure working with you.

I also want to thank you, dear reader. Thank you for walking through this Advent season with me. Thank you for trusting me and for holding some of my hurt too. I'm so sorry for the pain and loss that you know, and I'm praying for you. May you continue to keep a gaze fixed on Jesus and his goodness. The path might be difficult, but he's walking with you, and we're all heading home.

Printed in Great Britain
by Amazon